MEDICAL
SECOND
OPINION
How, When & Why

A Patient's Perspective

MEDICAL SECOND OPINION
How, When & Why

A Patient's Perspective

Dr Prahlad K. Sethi

MD, FAAN

STERLING PAPERBACKS
An imprint of
Sterling Publishers (P) Ltd.
Regd. Office: A-59, Okhla Industrial Area, Phase-II,
New Delhi-110020. CIN: U22110PB1964PTC002569
Tel: 26387070, 26386209; Fax: 91-11-26383788
E-mail: mail@sterlingpublishers.com
www.sterlingpublishers.com

Medical: Second Opinion How, When and Why
© 2015, Dr Prahlad K. Sethi
ISBN 978 81 207 9653 9

All rights are reserved.
No part of this publication may be reproduced, stored in a retrieval system or transmitted, in any form or by any means, mechanical, photocopying, recording or otherwise, without prior written permission of the author.

Cartoons designed by
Rabindra Choudhary

Printed in India
Printed and Published by Sterling Publishers Pvt. Ltd.,
New Delhi-110020.

Dedicated to

To the Art of Medicine

To my mentors Prof. Baldev Singh (AIIMS, New Delhi) and Prof. Bernard Smith (SUNY, New York,) for making me a well-rounded neurologist with a humane touch

To my parents Prakash and Veeran, for teaching me compassion, love and the importance of hard work

To my wife Shashi, for always being there to lean on

To my children Neetika and Nitin, for all the love and beauty they have brought to our lives

To all my exceptional Associates, Friends and, foremost, my Patients, for taking the time to teach, support and accept me.

Foreword

Professor P. K. Sethi has written this fascinating book *Medical: Second Opinion: How, When and Why,* which describes the thinking of doctors when dealing with their patients and the feelings of patients when facing their doctors. Drawing on his long experience as a doctor and a neurologist, supported by an excellent capacity for observation and intuition, Prof. Sethi, with his sensitivity and innate empathy for the patient, has written a book which needs to be read by practising doctors, general physicians and specialists, as well as by the lay public and also by the planners and thought leaders in the field of delivery of healthcare.

In simple language, he picks out examples from his wealth of experience to paint on a broad canvas the many facets which go into what is commonly described as Second Opinion. How do doctors react when their patients request or inform them that they have decided to ask for a second opinion? What are the reasons for asking to see another doctor? Can there be a set of criteria which should be fulfilled before going in for a second opinion? All these and several other issues which affect the decisions patients have to make regularly are discussed in this book. Prof. Sethi has drawn freely from the actual cases he has dealt with to illustrate the points made out by him. His empathy towards patients, his open mind free of dogma, his eye for detail and his sensitive observations of the flow of human life make this a must-read book.

Throughout the book, suggestions have been made, without any confrontation, as to how all people can get more out of life. The book is full of nuggets, which are true, though sometimes surprising.

"Many doctors are egoists. They believe that no other doctor is more knowledgeable than them in their area of specialization."

"Somewhere in this maddening world of technology, the doctor of today has become more a manager of technology and less a doctor."

"Treating a patient needs not only an understanding of his or her disease, but also an understanding of the patient's psyche."

I have picked these three observations from the early pages of the book. The book is full of such insights, so very important today when there is a growing disillusionment of the public over modern technology, over doctors lacking a human touch and over deterioration of the bonds between the doctor and the patient.

There are not many books written by an Indian doctor on the behavioural patterns of our patients and doctors. This book fulfils the need for such a book. It is written with sensitivity, keeping in mind the way we are brought up and our thinking. Prof. Sethi has however drawn also from his international experience. He deserves our gratitude for letting the patient, the public and the practitioner have a glimpse of what goes on behind the screen.

New Delhi **Professor Ranjit Roy Chaudhury**
23 September, 2014   M.B.B.S., D. Phil. (Oxon), FRCP (Edin),
FAMS, FNA (Ind. Med.),
FIMSA, D.Sc. (Hon. Causa)
National Professor of Pharmacology (NAMS)
Adviser to the Union Minister (GoI) for Health & Family Welfare

Introduction

A Google search on second opinion in medicine reveals that there are no established guidelines available to a patient.

When patients face a disease, most are ill-equipped to cope with it. Some patients are mortally scared when sitting in front of an imposing doctor. They worry about the disease and how it might affect them. The doctor, seated on other the other side of the table, should be able to feel the anxiety and fear which grips the mind of the patient when the disease is persistent and causing problems. It is important to understand the patient's thought process.

When you are sick, you are vulnerable, you are worried about how the disease will affect you. Will it be a brief period of suffering or a chronic, debilitating disease? Then, there are apprehensions about the doctor and his diagnosis. You may suffer from the "white coat-syndrome" or you may be the kind of a person who plays down the symptoms and adopts a false sense of bravado. As each patient behaves differently, the doctor has the responsibility to not only diagnosis the illness, but also understand the thought process of the patient.

Most patients are generally satisfied with the recommended treatment prescribed by their doctor. They do not feel that a second opinion is necessary. Of those who feel uneasy with their doctor's recommendation, many suppress their doubts and proceed with the recommended therapy.

However many patients do seek a second opinion for a variety of reasons and for some the experience is not pleasant. Dr Robert Klitzma, in an essay in 2008, confesses, "When I went for a second opinion, my internist got mad." A physician with lymphoma recently told me, "I went for a second opinion and my doctor behaved as if I was his lover and had cheated on him."

These reactions, while extreme, are far from uncommon. Second opinions have, undoubtedly, saved many lives and have gained importance with the growing public focus on medical errors and the availability of the internet. After all, Dr Google is now available anytime, anyplace, to render his opinion! While second opinions can lead to awkward situations in a doctor-patient relationship, surprisingly, little is known or written about this.

Not much research has been done on how often second opinions are taken; how, when, and why patients decide to obtain them; the obstacles faced by patients and physicians alike; and how these obstacles are overcome. I have interviewed physicians who themselves were patients, some with serious illnesses and who have thus faced both sides of the situation. They all felt that the medical professional etiquette or systems often operated against second opinion and that it affected their optimal treatment.

Misdiagnosis is not uncommon in medicine. Sixty-five per cent of cases presented in Medical Grand

Introduction

Rounds (Grand Rounds are meetings where the case-history of a complicated case of a patient is presented to an audience consisting of doctors, residents and medical students) to experts were originally misdiagnosed or mistreated.

Readers may be surprised to learn how often doctors seek informal second opinions concerning their own patients. Doctors frequently kerbside other doctors to discuss a particularly challenging case — a patient with an unusual presentation of a common disease or a common presentation of a rare disease. They routinely discuss difficult cases in conferences and seek a consensus opinion. Once or twice a week someone in my practice will send out an email asking others in the group to provide an opinion on a challenging MRI or electrocardiogram. I think most doctors have a healthy understanding of their own limitations — at least I hope so.

In this book I have made a humble and, hopefully, a light hearted attempt to tell patients how, when, and why to seek a second opinion. Whenever feasible, I have given anecdotes, many of them personal, to explain my point. Being a neurologist, most examples are from a neurological point of view. But similar situation occur in general medicine and other specialties, too.

Cast of recurring characters:
Shashi-my wife
Neetika-my daughter
Nitin-my son

Contents

Foreword 7

Introduction 11

1. Second Opinion—Doctor's and Patient's Perspective 17
2. Get a Doctor! 21
3. How to Decide If Your Doctor Is the Right One for You 24
4. Living in a World Ruled by Technology 26
5. Second Opinion for Confirming Self-Belief 32
6. You Are My Doctor—You Take the Call for Me! 35
7. Second Opinion and Alternate Medicine 39
8. Seeking Opinion in the Search of a Diagnostic Label 43
9. Second Opinion Sought by Well-Wishers to Fulfil a Personal Agenda 46
10. Second Opinion for an Incurable Disease—In Search of Hope 51
11. Unity in Diversity—Patients Are the Same All over the World 52
12. When Not to Seek a Second Opinion 54

13. Second Opinion—Setting the Ball Rolling   57
14. Preparing Your Case for a Second Opinion   59
15. From Whom to Seek a Second Opinion?   61
16. Choosing the Right Consultant   62
17. Who is the Best Physician?   66
18. When to Take a Second Opinion?   68
19. Second Opinion in Surgery or Intervention   88
20. Multiple Second Opinions and Medical
    Shopping   93
21. Second Opinion—Faith and Closure   99

1

Second Opinion—Doctor's and Patient's Perspective

One day, 30 years ago, when I was doing my Residency in neurology at Buffalo, New York, USA, one of my attending physicians, Dr Nichloson Zurecki, surprised me by his comment. Nick, as he was called, was attached to Meyer Memorial Hospital where he enjoyed admission privileges (admitting privilege is the right of the doctor to admit patients to a particular hospital). He used to teach once in a week when doing the rounds in the hospital.

He was always cheerful and I knew he was doing very well in practice. One day he said to me, "Dr Sethi, I have arrived. I am happy with my practice and feel confident. Now I don't mind if my patient asks for a second opinion. In fact, sometimes I suggest that they seek one. I do this in cases of diagnostic difficulties or incurable diseases. I give them the names of four or five neurologists in New York and ask them to choose one. I do this so that they do not fall in the wrong hands. The doctors I recommend have a high professional standing and an impeccable reputation."

At that time I was young and still learning the nuances of neurology. I did not understand the exact meaning of Nick's statement "I have arrived." Maturity does not necessarily come with age, since it is a state of the mind. A doctor has to be mature and confident and not mind when a patient seeks another doctor for a second opinion. Age has nothing to do with the confidence a doctor needs to possess to suggest to his patients to take a second opinion. Much later in life, I realized that many doctors are egoists. They believe that no other doctor is more knowledgeable than them in their area of specialization. Many feel hurt if their patient asks for a second opinion or seeks one without their permission.

Second opinion? Nawab Sahib, eh?

Second Opinion – Doctor's and Patient's Perspective

Very few doctors have the confidence in themselves to suggest that their patient seek a second opinion. As a result, many patients do so without informing their doctor in case he feels hurt or becomes vindictive.

Many times when the patient goes for a second opinion, he acts as if the doctor he is consulting is the first one he has approached. After the consultation, at times, unable to contain himself, the patient blurts out that his primary doctor also gave the same advice or rendered a different opinion!

An intelligent doctor is one who remembers that there may be a different diagnosis which he may have overlooked. So, sooner or later, a doctor has to become mature enough so as not to get upset if his patient goes for a second opinion and should be willing to discuss the outcome of the second opinion with his patient.

There should be transparency in the doctor-patient relationship. The patient will respect and appreciate the doctor for his open-mindedness. It is only then that the doctor has, as Dr Nick said, truly arrived.

In the meantime, what should the patient do? He does not know whether his doctor will encourage him to seek a second opinion.

The patient should have guidelines about when he should seek a second opinion. He should consider the following:

I. Is there a need for second opinion?
II. When should he take a second opinion?
III. When should he not take a second opinion?
IV. How to seek a second opinion—preparation of the medical case report.
V. From whom to seek second opinion—seeking the right consultant.
VI. What to do with the second opinion—sharing it with the primary doctor.

This short book answers these as well as other questions which, no doubt, prevail in the patient's mind. It is my humble attempt to convey both the patient's and the doctor's perspectives. I hope you enjoy reading it.

2
Get a Doctor!

A. J. Cronin, the famous doctor-turned-author, describes an event. He was invited by his publisher for dinner. He noted that the maid, while serving food, was limping. He offered to examine her knee. She firmly, yet politely, turned down his offer as she preferred to go to her village the following day to be examined by her doctor. "My doctor" is what she said.

In England, there exists the concept of a GP (General Physician) or a family doctor. As super-specialty hospitals and specialists increase in number, the GP concept is becoming extinct. In the USA, there is a concept of the primary care physician (PCP), which sounds good, but somehow does not equate mentally to the GP or "my doctor". It may sound strange, but it is true that a good GP or "family doctor" is difficult to find nowadays. In this age of specialists and super-specialists, the GP is a vanishing breed.

Recently, a prominent lawyer of Delhi asked me to get him a GP. I approached a doctor, whom I knew, for this purpose, but he politely declined. I enquired the reason for his refusal. He said, "Your lawyer friend will call me for a house call and I will end up taking the blood pressure of all his family members and even the servants. Most rich people are poor paymasters."

It is very difficult, indeed, to find a capable GP. Many good doctors refuse to take up this role since the financial rewards are meagre. So if you have a good GP, do not lose him; give him the respect he deserves and do not take undue advantage of him. And if you do not have one, do spend the time and effort to find one and then build a lasting relationship with him. A good doctor is worth his weight in gold.

There are times when everyone needs a doctor, even specialist doctors themselves! Dr Frank, a famous gastroenterologist and hepatologist, fell sick and was diagnosed to have hepatobiliary cancer. In spite of his daughter and son-in-law being in the same specialty, he consulted many other specialists to find a cure for his problem. As time went by, his frustration increased. He expressed his dissatisfaction to one of his close friends. His friend's advice was, "Frank, get a doctor!" What his friend meant was that Dr Frank needed a GP who could understand his problems, take a holistic view of the symptoms, and whose recommendations he would trust and accept.

We all need to have a doctor in whom we have faith. He will be our friend in need, indeed even our saviour. If you already have a doctor who is like a friend and philosopher, then consider yourself extremely fortunate. Or else, spare no effort trying to find one. One of my patients told me his prescription for well-being. He said that whenever he moved to a new town, his first

Get a Doctor!

priority was to find a good doctor. He said, "To be able to survive in any town or metropolitan city, you need to have a good doctor, a smart lawyer and an honest cop as your friend."

All second opinions are double charges!

3

How to Decide If Your Doctor Is the Right One for You

How do you decide if your doctor is the right doctor for you? My Chief of Neurology, Prof. Bernard H. Smith, during my Residency training in neurology, gave me an excellent piece of advice. He said, "If I fall sick, I would not like to be looked after by a clever doctor but by a wise one." To determine why you are getting spells of giddiness, a clever doctor will say, "Let us do a four-vessel angiography of the brain and the heart." A wise doctor, on the other hand, will listen to your medical history carefully, ask you probing questions, give you a thorough physical examination, and formulate a list of diagnostic possibilities. He will then conduct relevant investigations to confirm or refute the diagnostic possibilities.

The following example, a case from my patient files, will illustrate the point. A 42-year-old CEO of a firm used to have giddy spells, always in his office, and mostly in the winter months. He was admitted to a renowned hospital for investigations and underwent a battery of tests, including EKG, echocardiogram (ECHO), treadmill stress test, tilt table, MRI of the brain with MR angiography, and EEG. The results were all normal. His doctors assured him that as he was getting his attacks in office, the cause was stress. That he would get the attacks only in the winters was not considered relevant and ignored. By this time, it was summer and his spells of giddiness stopped, adding to his belief that his doctors were right.

In the beginning of the winter the following year, he went to a tailor for getting new suits and shirts stitched. The tailor took all his measurements meticulously. He was quite satisfied, except when it came to the collar size. The CEO insisted that it measured 14½ inches, while the tailor insisted that it was 15. Ultimately, the tailor gave up, saying, "As you wish, but I feel that in winter, when you go out wearing a tie, you may get dizzy spells due to the tight collar exerting pressure on the blood vessels in the neck."

A wise doctor would have paid attention to the occurrence of the dizzy spells only in the winter months while the CEO was in his office, formally dressed in a shirt and tie. The above example illustrates the thoroughness with which a doctor should analyse the case histories of his patients.

So how do you determine if a doctor is the right one for you? Unfortunately this is not as easy as looking up a name in the yellow pages. It is important that you do a bit of research. A good place to start is to look up the professional profile of the doctor on the internet. Does he specialize in the disease that ails you? Is he board certified (a process by which a physician demonstrates mastery of the skills in his area of specialization)? Recommendation from family and friends can be invaluable in finding the right doctor. Hospital websites are helpful resources too.

4
Living in a World Ruled by Technology

Naturopathy by modern machines!

I go for a morning walk to a sports facility near my home. The Asiad Village Sports Complex is a huge complex which was constructed for the 1982 Asian Games. There is a running track; a gymnasium; tennis, badminton, and squash courts; an Olympic sized swimming pool; hockey and football fields. Naturally, this complex draws many sports and fitness lovers. Seeing the large number of visitors, yoga gurus and marketers of health foods have set up shops there. Some entrepreneurs have also opened an Ayurveda and Naturopathy clinic.

One day, as I was entering the complex, my eyes fell on a large billboard at the entrance gate. It boldly proclaimed, "NAJRUOPATHY WITH MODERN MACHINES." It amused me. Besides the obvious spelling error, it seemed to have a contradiction. It made me wonder what they did with their modern machines. Probably they gave enema under hydrolytic pressure! I guess naturopathy, with the use modern gadgets, was a smart marketing gimmick to catch the attention of a gullible public.

In the era of MRI and CT scans, modern medicine is now technology driven. For the first time I saw that even alternate medicine, or rather complementary medicine as it is called now, was also gadget dependent. Why should naturopathy, traditionally meaning living with nature, need modern machines?

It is true that, over the years, several major breakthroughs and innovations have taken place in modern medicine. These include breakthroughs in investigation techniques in all specialties, such as cardiology, internal medicine, neurology, neurosurgery, nephrology and so on. Some well-deserved Nobel prizes have been awarded for CT and MRI scans. Echocardiography, angiography, Holter and MUGA scans, all play a role in modern cardiology.

Thirty years ago, none of us could have imagined that one day we would be able to see a living brain through machines like CT and MRI. Endoscopy has revolutionized gastroenterology, both diagnostic and therapeutically. Procedures like cardiac angiography and angioplasty have revolutionized the therapeutic approaches to cardiac diseases.

Dialysis has saved countless lives. Transplantation of kidney, liver, lung, etc., has given a new life to the critically ill. Modern equipment and advances in diagnosis and management of eye diseases has made eye surgery techniques safer. Bone marrow transplantation, advances in genetics and molecular biology, have opened new vistas. Antibiotics, immunoglobulin, plasmapheresis, and new drugs for cancer have unimaginable therapeutic possibilities. Advances in genetics have brought in a revolution. Breakthrough in stem-cell technology, although at present mostly experimental, has huge potential.

These advances have been achieved over the years by dedicated men and women working in the field of medicine and allied specialties. No praise is enough for them. However, somewhere in this maddening world of technology, the doctor of today has become more a manager of technology and less a doctor.

Looks like you have a fracture. But get all these tests done, anyway!

Medicine has made tremendous technological and scientific advances, but it still cannot be a called a "perfect science" because it is not only a science, but also an art. Doctors have to deal with human beings of different genetic make-ups, different socio-cultural backgrounds, different food habits, different mentalities, different psyches, different ethnic groups and religious affiliations, and with different beliefs and upbringing. Thus, the same disease may manifest differently in different people. Therefore, treating a patient needs not only an understanding of his or her disease, but also an understanding of the patient's psyche. Then, and only then, can the doctor treat the patient appropriately. So doctors have to remember that investigations, although invaluable, cannot replace a good history, thorough clinical examination and valuable details of the patient and his mental and thought processes.

The "machine age" has also changed the patient's psychological behaviour. Patients have developed more trust and faith in investigations and the use of modern gadgetry than in the doctor's judgement. One day, I asked one of my colleagues, a physiotherapist, "Why are you spending more time in stimulation and machine-oriented techniques rather than in teaching proper exercises to your patient affected with stroke and paralysis?" His frank reply was that patients preferred the use of machines and many were not willing to go through vigorous or intensive physiotherapy.

As a senior (not in years but in experience!) neurologist, I frequently get patients who have already been seen by one or two other neurologists. A patient of epilepsy arrives bringing with him reports of many MRIs and other investigations. I find below-average notes from the doctors describing the patient's epileptic attack. It is well known that the diagnosis of epilepsy is clinical, based on a good eyewitness account of the patient's seizure. A positive EEG may support the diagnosis, but a negative EEG does not rule it out. The EEG is positive only if, at the time of recording, epileptic discharges are captured. As epilepsy is episodic, an EEG may be normal but the patient may still have epilepsy. An MRI may show the structural cause of epilepsy, if any. More often, the MRI is also normal. When I ask the patient or family the details of the attack, many seem to get irritated. They feel, "Why is this doctor asking so many questions and cross-examining? He is wasting our time. Why can't he just examine the MRI and EEG and diagnose?" The patient feels that he has spent money on the MRI and I am wasting his time by asking him questions about his seizure. In other words, the patient has more faith in machines and tests (the more expensive the better!) than in his doctor.

The patient should understand that a good doctor invariably spends time to get a detailed history by asking probing questions, frequently akin to a cross-examination, and by a thorough physical exam. Approximately 90 per cent medical diagnoses are made in this manner. They are clinical and not based on tests, no matter how expensive. Tests frequently help to confirm the diagnosis already made. An experienced and wise doctor chooses the correct and necessary investigations to prove or disprove his diagnosis.

At this juncture, I will quote another case. A 45-year-old patient, with a history of back pain for two months and mild-to-moderate weakness in the legs, came to me with his MRIs. After taking his history, I found that he was having sensory loss at the level of the umbilicus. I asked him to get a new MRI focusing at the thoracic

(D6-D7) level. He said he already had a MRI of the lumbar region and it was reported normal. The reason for missing the correct diagnosis became abundantly clear. Subsequent MRI focusing at the proper level revealed a compressive lesion due to a meningioma. Surgical removal of the same completely cured him of his problem.

Another patient got admitted to a university teaching hospital with fever and excruciatingly severe headache. Blood investigations and MRI (brain) were normal. As she was being sent back home with painkillers for the headache, it was noted by an observant and wise doctor that she had a slight stiffness in the neck. A lumbar puncture (spinal tap) was done and the spinal fluid revealed that she was suffering from meningitis, which was treated with appropriate therapy and she made a complete recovery. So what she needed was a careful examination and well-directed investigations to confirm the clinical diagnosis.

Hence, patients should be aware that tests and investigations are a means to an end, not an end by themselves. Technology in the right hands (an intelligent doctor), when used in the right fashion, helps to confirm or refute a diagnosis.

5

Second Opinion for Confirming Self-Belief

Before seeking a second opinion, it is advisable that the patient sits in a quiet place and tries to analyse dispassionately what his motives for seeking a second opinion are. Does he have doubts about the diagnosis? Is the suggested treatment too cumbersome? Is it against his beliefs? Is the suggested procedure (surgery) avoidable? Does seeking a second opinion seem logical and appeal to common sense?

Each of us, while growing up, has certain beliefs about our body, diseases in general and different therapies. These beliefs and ideas are influenced or reinforced by our upbringing, education, socio-economic background, cultural and religious influences, and even the country we grow up in. When I was doing Residency in neurology, this fact was bought to my notice by Prof. Bernard H. Smith. Prof. Smith was a Scotsman who first trained in psychiatry and then neurology in Montreal, Canada. Although he settled in the United States and was now a professor of neurology, he was still British at heart and somewhat uncomfortable with the way medicine was practiced in the United States. One day, during rounds, he asked me to examine the abdomen of a patient, a 38-year-old woman who worked in the same hospital as a receptionist and was admitted for investigation of pain in the neck. Her abdomen bore several surgical scars, one from where the gall bladder was removed, one from the removal of a kidney and another from the removal of her uterus. Prof. Smith sarcastically remarked that in USA, there was a great practice. If an organ was not functioning properly, why keep it? Remove it! "Take away the disease from its root." He said, "Dr Sethi, interestingly, most patients are also pro-surgery." He added, "Americans will get their heart removed and replaced, if it was covered by insurance." So in some western countries people believe in surgery and consider surgery curative.

In contrast, when I started practising in India, I found that patients, by and large, were scared of surgery, even if it was absolutely essential and life-saving. I know of several patients who were told that they have cancer for which they would need radical surgery to prevent its spread. They kept on seeking second opinions till they found a "clever" doctor — one who could read their mind and agree to treat them without surgery. Such patients generally prefer practitioners of alternate medicine as these practioners never recommend surgery. They start taking the prescribed alternate therapy medicines. Some of them start to feel better initially, probably because of a placebo effect. It is known that as much as 30 per cent of patients feel symptomatically better because of having faith in the treatment. A medicine only works if a doctor and patient have faith in it.

As a doctor, this is my opinion. If you want a second opinion, ask Dr Google!

In the case of a patient who had jaundice because of cancer in the hepato-biliary region, his condition worsened. Frantic, he sought the opinion of the doctor he had consulted initially and was told that his cancer had now spread and was out of control and that he was beyond surgery, and only chemotherapy was an option. The doctor felt bad for him as initially the disease was "confined" and surgery would have been curative.

Patients sometimes seek a second opinion to confirm their strongly held beliefs. These beliefs, in my opinion, are deeply rooted in their psyche, modified by educational and cultural factors. They determine whether they are for or against surgery, for or against complementary medicine (Ayurveda, Chinese medicine, etc.) and for or against taking medications.

6

You Are My Doctor—You Take the Call for Me!

My father called me on my mobile phone one afternoon. His message was brief, stating he was not feeling well and had jaundice. I asked him to come immediately to my hospital and took him to see a gastroenterologist. He examined my 78-year-old father, reviewed the blood tests and reassured both of us that it was only a case of viral hepatitis (inflammation of the liver) and prescribed medicines. I felt reassured, as did my father.

But three days later my father rang me early morning to say that his jaundice was worsening and that he had no appetite. I asked him to come to the hospital again for an ultrasound of the abdomen. It was shocking, indeed, to learn that he actually had cancer of the pancreas, which was blocking the flow of bile, causing jaundice. Of all the cancers, pancreatic cancer has one of the most dismal prognosis. As it progresses, the jaundice keeps getting worse, reducing appetite and causing severe abdominal pain and discomfort. I was completely shaken and taken aback by the news and tried to convey it to my father in a gentle manner. My father, always a stoic man, took the news with a straight face, making me wonder whether he comprehended the gravity of his ailment.

One of my father's friends was admitted to the same hospital at the same time and my father insisted on visiting him. I tried to talk him out of this as I did not want his friends to know that he was just diagnosed with pancreatic cancer. With great difficulty, I was able to convince him to go home with one of my nephews. Much later did I come to know that instead of going home, he insisted on going to a sweet shop in Karol Bagh to savour his favourite dessert *rabri* (an Indian sweet).

My father was raised in the North West Frontier Province (now in Pakistan), a region inhabited by the Pathans. He had imbibed many of their characteristics. Physically, he was a short man, but he more than made up for it with his tough determination. He came for a well-to-do family, who migrated to India after partition and went through very difficult times. But he never gave up and put us all through college. Over the next week I learnt that he had phoned all his friends and relatives (believe me when I say we have a large extended family) and informed them all of his ailment

Death is inevitable but one hopes for dying with dignity.

You have to take the call.

Nobody wants to get involved in a fight; the art of war is to win a war without a fight.

But when fight is inevitable, you should stand firm and catch the bull by the horn.

and that his days were numbered. This was done as a matter of fact, with no sorrow and without the desire to seek anyone's sympathy. I, on the other hand, avoided talking to anyone about his cancer.

Shortly thereafter, he was admitted to the hospital and the gastroenterologist put in a shunt to relieve his jaundice. With the jaundice gone, his appetite retuned and he started feeling better. In the meantime, I consulted numerous gastroenterologists, surgeons and oncologists (cancer specialists). All of them said that surgery was a major undertaking, without any significant beneficial gains with respect to prolonging longevity. Life expectancy is only five to six months in pancreatic cancer, in spite of all interventions. The oncologist insisted on starting chemotherapy (anti-cancer medications), which causes intolerable side-effects. I was confused how to proceed further and, after explaining the situation to my father, asked him what I should do. He surprised me by his one-liner, "You are my doctor Prahlad, you decide for me."

After that he was perfectly calm and at peace. He had left the decision to me, to his doctor. I was taken aback by the courage and confidence he had reposed in me. I decided not to subject him to further chemotherapy and to pursue palliative care. During the last six months of his life, he met all his friends, visited all the places he wanted to, ate all the food he loved. One evening he complained of sudden chest pain and died of a heart attack.

I learnt a big lesson from my father. When faced with a terminal illness, he had taken medical opinions and then left the decision to his doctor. He had placed his trust in me, his doctor and his son, to do the right thing for him. I also learnt we all handle and react to bad medical news differently. Some like to confide in their family and friends, others prefer to keep it private.

You have amnesia? OK! Remember, I gave you the second opinion!

7
Second Opinion and Alternate Medicine

After completing Residency training in neurology in the United States, I returned to India in 1973 and was assigned to Army Hospital, Lucknow. The hospital had 800 beds, with the neurology centre comprising 75 beds. At a young age of 33, I was heading the Neurology Department of Command Hospital, Lucknow. One eminent doctor, who had served there during World War II, was Prof. Denny Brown. Even my chief in United States, Prof. Bernard Smith, had served in the British Army and had been stationed in nearby Kanpur. The hospital library was home to some good medical journals and books. It felt great to be there and having just returned from the USA, I felt I knew everything. But I had a lot to learn.

One day an officer brought his wife to see me. She was suffering from epilepsy and after relevant investigations, I prescribed an anticonvulsant (anti-seizure medicine). As they were leaving, the officer asked me, "Doctor, can she take her Homeopathic medicines along with this medicine?" I politely replied that since I did not know anything about Homeopathy, I could not answer his question. He retorted, "Everybody knows that the two systems of medicines cannot go hand in hand. Why cannot you give me a straightforward 'Yes' or 'No' answer?" I felt a little helpless and chose to remain silent.

Over the years I have learnt a lot about how to handle this situation. India is a vast country, home to many systems of medicines and medical theories. There is Homeopathy, Unani, Ayurveda, Naturopathy, Tibetan medicine, herbal medicine, Vastu (an ancient doctrine which consists of precepts born out of a traditional Hindu view about cosmos and how the laws of nature affect human dwellings), acupuncture and Reiki, to name just a few. Then there are the faith healers — pundits, ojhas (medicine men who chase away evil spirits), maulvis (Muslin preachers) and many others. The various systems and faith healers have their own interpretation of a disease and its cure.

One day, I bumped into a leading pulmonologist in the corridors of our hospital. The love of his country had brought him back, after spending 14 years in the USA in a leading hospital in New York. He said to me, "PK, you also did your training in USA and are at ease practising here in India. I, on the other hand, after three years working here, have decided to go back to USA." I asked him why he wanted to leave. He said, "There are two problems I face here — one is the doctor problem and the other is the patient problem." He explained further.

The doctor problem was that medical specialists were always undermining and running one another down. A doctor would look at the prescription given by another doctor, smile wryly and comment to the patient, "Oh! Did he really prescribe that?" But worse than that, he said, was the patient problem. Patients would frequently complain that they were not feeling better even after taking his prescribed medication. It took my friend (the pulmonologist) some time to figure out the cause of this lack of efficacious response to medication. Patients would frequently modify the dose of the prescribed medicine according to their beliefs. When confronted, they would simply say, "I reduced the medicine dose to one tablet daily instead of three as I am also taking Homeopathy pills for this." In India, my friend felt, alternate medicine frequently replaced allopathic medicine. This was the cause of his frustration.

Some practitioners of alternate medicine have a smart business strategy. They tell the patient who seeks a second opinion from them to continue taking the allopathic medicines prescribed by their "regular" doctor and to also take the alternate medicine concurrently. As the patient is leaving their clinic, as an afterthought, they add, "As you know, alternate medicine doesn't have any side-effects." A clever move indeed, I say! If the patient improved, the credit goes to the alternate medicine practitioner and if there are side-effects, then the blame is assigned to the allopathic medicine prescribed by the "regular" doctor. A win-win situation for the practitioner of alternate medicine!

I am not running down any particular system of medicine, but merely trying to highlight the beliefs and behaviour of the patients. To practise good medicine, accountability is a must. Some alternate medicines are known to contain heavy metals and even high dosage of steroids, which can cause serious side-effects. Practitioners of alternate systems of medicine should be held to the same standards of accountability as a licensed medical doctor.

8

Seeking Opinion in the Search of a Diagnostic Label

Nitin, my son, is a neurologist and an epileptologist (specialist in seizure disorders), working in a prestigious academic centre and hospital in New York City. A while ago, a young lady came to him seeking a second opinion. She was experiencing episodes of abnormal movements wherein she would shake her limbs erratically and collapse, but in such manner so as not to hurt herself.

A concern for seizures was raised. While in his office, she had her typical "seizure" right in front of him, shaking violently and falling rather dramatically on to the couch. Any attempt to open her eyes was resisted and she would keep them tightly shut. When the eyes were opened, she would roll them up to avoid making eye contact. Her event fitted the description of a non-epileptic event, at times referred to as a pseudoseizure (an attack resembling an epileptic seizure but having purely psychological causes, lacking the electroencephalographic changes of epilepsy and sometimes able to be stopped by an act of will). She had already consulted a couple of neurologists and undergone multiple EEG tests and MRI scans, all of which had been reported normal. She insisted admission to the hospital to get another video EEG study, which confirmed the reported events were indeed non-epileptic seizures. On being told that her events were psychological, she became upset and threatened to sue my son and the hospital.

Some patients seek second opinions in search of a diagnostic label. They want to find a doctor who can assign a diagnostic label to their disease and frequently get upset when told there is "nothing wrong with them" or it is "only anxiety and stress".

Neurologists, like Prof. Stanley Fahn, a world renowned neurologist specializing in movement disorders, frequently encounter patients with psychogenic movement disorders. Many get very upset when told that their problems are psychogenic in origin. How do smart neurologists deal with such patients? They run the necessary tests to first confirm the diagnosis and then, after acknowledging the problem ("Yes, something is wrong and you need help"), they involve a psychiatrist as a part of the treating team. The psychiatrist helps to address the underlying issues, such as anxiety, depression and stress.

As a neurologist I see many patients who suffer from anxiety and depression, presenting somatic complaints such as chronic headache, body aches, stomach issues and even non-epileptic seizures and movement disorders. I prefer to use words such as, "Luckily, your hard disk (brain) is fine, but the software (mind) is faulty." This satisfies the patient's desire of having a diagnostic label attached to their complaint and makes it easier for me to treat them. Telling the patient that all his complaints are psychogenic makes them angry (So, Dr Sethi, you are telling me that I am crazy?) and drives them away.

Prof. Bernard Smith used to put this in a different way. He was taking care of the patriarch of a big business family. Whenever confronted with a difficult situation, this gentleman would fall sick, saying his peptic ulcer had flared up. This was his "safety valve" to get out of the stressful situation. Dr Smith's advice was simple, "Do not take away his safety valve." A "clever" doctor, on the other hand, may not understand the importance of this safety valve and declare, after conducting an endoscopy, that there was no ulcer at all. A wise doctor like Dr Smith understood the complete situation and, after endoscopy, provided the patriarch with a face-saving solution. "Although at present there no active ulcer, I found his stomach mucosa inflamed and have advised rest," he declared. So while understanding the patient's psychology is important for the treating physician, patients and caregivers, too, need to understand their desire to have a diagnostic label attached to their complaints. Many a time the reason for seeking a second opinion is this search for a diagnostic label and, in my opinion, attaching a new diagnostic label or taking away an established one (diagnosing a neurological disease) can, at times, be very helpful if done tactfully.

9

Second Opinion Sought by Well-Wishers to Fulfil a Personal Agenda

Sometimes second opinion is sought by persons who are neither legal guardians nor primary caregivers of the patient. Both the doctor and the patient have to be careful of such well-wishers as their motives may be suspect or they may harbour their own agenda. A few examples will help to illustrate my point.

One day I received a call from Dr Sama, the Chairman of Sir Ganga Ram Hospital where I am a senior consultant neurologist. Dr Sama informed me that the son of my patient, Mrs R, who was admitted under my care, was very upset about the care given to his mother and that he had lodged a complaint with the hospital administration and requested a second opinion. Mrs R's son had come all the way from New York, USA, on being informed by relatives that his mother was very sick and admitted to the hospital with a stroke and pneumonia (chest infection). Apparently, he was very well placed in America and was settled there. I informed Dr Sama that, contrary to initial evaluation, Mrs R was actually doing quite well. The pneumonia had cleared, but the stroke had left her weak on one side of her body. The son had come from USA on 15 days leave, thinking that his mother was critical and may not survive. The reason for his unhappiness with our care and request for a second opinion was that now that his mother was recovering slowly, he would have to delay his return to America.

In another case, I received a call one night from a lady whose father was critically ill and in a comatose condition in the intensive care unit (ICU). On the phone, she seemed anxious and upset and wanted me to see her father that night itself. I wondered whether my junior doctors had forgotten to mention this case to me when I had taken my rounds in the ICU that morning. These thoughts were disturbing me and I was not relishing driving in the middle of the night to see this patient. As I talked to her over the phone, I realized that her father was not admitted under my care, but was under another Internal Medicine consultant. Apparently, I had seen her father during his previous admission to the hospital three month ago, for a stroke. I felt relieved and told her that I could not come that night but would be happy to see him first thing in the morning. She pleaded, saying that I could take any amount of fee, but I should come and see her father immediately. She said she was not satisfied with the present doctor under whom her father was admitted. I explained to her that, as per medical ethics and hospital rules, I could not see her father without a formal request from the primary consultant and promised her that I would be happy to see him the next day, if requested by his primary consultant.

Next day, after receiving a formal request, I saw her father and then informed the daughter that her father had suffered a devastating brainstem stroke and was unlikely to survive. She implored me to make him "conscious" even for a very short time. Three days later, I bumped into the primary consultant and he informed me that the patient had died that same day. He said that although the daughter had seemed so concerned at that time, she had not yet come and claim her father's body from the hospital mortuary, even after three days. Later, we came to know that she only wanted him to recover long enough to change his will in her favour.

Second opinion sought out of feelings of guilt

Mrs N was admitted to the stroke unit with a massive stroke. A guarded prognosis regarding her recovery was given to her husband, who was satisfied with the care being administered to her. Then Mrs N's daughter, from out of town, arrived. She had not visited her 78-year-old mother for the past five or six years, although her mother had not been keeping good health. Mrs N had a history of poorly controlled diabetes, hypertension, a mild stroke and heart disease. As soon as the daughter arrived, she started to ask questions from my team of doctors. Not satisfied with the answers she received, she said she intended to seek a second opinion from a leading doctor in USA. My junior neurologist felt upset and disheartened by her attitude. I told him of my experiences and placated him by saying that the daughter's remarks had nothing to do with our competence. She was feeling guilty about neglecting her mother and her way of mitigating that guilt was by seeking a second opinion.

During my Residency in USA, I learnt a valuable lesson. I had an 80-year-old lady admitted under my care with a stroke. She was in a vegetative state and was awaiting placement in a nursing home. The waiting list at the nursing home was rather long. One night, suddenly, she died. Next day her six-foot-two son located me in the hospital and threatened me with litigation for neglecting his mother. By now I had been advised by my fellow residents that my mild Indian demeanour was ineffective and I should assert my authority. Looking him in the eye, I politely but firmly asked him why he had not cared to visit his ailing mother even once over the past three months she had been in the hospital. To my surprise, he immediately quietened down, apologized and thanked me for looking after his mother. He mumbled that he had been busy with work and therefore unable to visit his mother, although he very much wanted to. I realized that he was feeling guilty and his initial outburst and threat to take me to court was only an attempt to transfer his guilt on to me.

Second opinion for medico-legal purposes

Mrs Singh, a 30-year-old pretty and smart lady, brought her husband to me for a second opinion. Her father accompanied them. Mr. Singh had been diagnosed with epilepsy and so they came to see me, carrying many EEGs and MRI scans. After going through the medical records, I assured her that her husband should do well as his epilepsy was due to a solitary neurocysticercosis cyst (an infection of the brain due to tapeworm and a rather common cause of seizures in India). Subsequently, they came to see me three more times and on each occasion her father paid my consultation fees. On the fourth visit, Mrs Singh appeared agitated and told me that the previous night her husband had a seizure during which he took out a sword and chased her from the second floor of the house to the first floor and then to the basement. She said she saved herself by hiding in the basement. Under these circumstances, she said she could not live with her husband anymore and wanted to apply for a divorce. She wanted me to appear on her behalf in court.

It was then that I caught on to her motive in seeking a second opinion from a senior neurologist like me. I politely told her that if ever summons in my name came from the court, I would support my patient, her husband, although her father had been paying my fees. I informed her that during a seizure, a patient can get agitated, but is unlikely to be so coordinated as to chase her down two floors into the basement.

10

Second Opinion for an Incurable Disease— In Search of Hope

Prof. Mathews of Oxford describes in his book *Practical Neurology* how to treat an incurable disease. While a disease such as cancer may be incurable, it can still be treated. There are many symptomatic treatments which alleviate patient discomfort and pain, improving their quality of life.

Many patients with incurable diseases seek a second opinion. Sometimes, this is in search of hope. *Maybe there is some cure out there which my doctor has not heard of.* While the decision to seek a second opinion under these circumstances is understandable, patients and their family members need to be careful that they are not misled by someone offering false hope. They should do their homework well and make sure that the treatment options they pursue are based on scientific merit.

11

Unity in Diversity–Patients Are the Same All over the World

In one of the earlier chapters, I said that different patients' reactions differ, even though they may be suffering from the same disease. Many factors play a role in this, including genetic, socioeconomic, cultural and religious factors and last, but not the least, education. But surprisingly, in one aspect all patients are similar. All patients seek hope when faced with a terminal illness. Many patients may express the desire to end their life, but the desire for life is also greatest when one is dying.

Mrs S, my wife's aunt, was suffering from asthma and chronic bronchitis for many years. Towards the end, she needed respiratory support and I remember her last words, "Give me back my breath and I'll show the world how to live."

One day, about 20 years ago, I received a call from a local nursing home, known as East West Nursing Home, to come and see an American patient. East West Nursing Home was popular with international patients.

The patient was suffering from AIDS. At that time AIDS was not well known in India and our experience with the disease was limited. My patient was in a serious condition. I could not resist asking his wife why she had brought him all the way from United States to India. There were hardly any treatment options available for AIDS in India at that time.

Her answer surprised me. "Doctor Sethi, don't you know that only in India a cure for AIDS exists?" Apparently one of her relatives, working in the American Embassy in New Delhi, had seen an advertisement in a local newspaper by a hakim (a practitioner of Unani medicine), claiming to have successfully treated and cured cases of cancer and AIDS. So it was hope for a cure which brought this American couple to India. Before that, I had only heard of wealthy Indians flying to the USA for medical treatment.

Nowadays, some Americans fly to China seeking stem cell treatment for various chronic incurable diseases, despite the fact that the US Food and Drug Administration has not approved stem cell therapy for these conditions. Hope for a cure is, indeed, a unifying factor, despite all our diversity.

A medicine works till you and your doctor have faith in it.

12

When Not to Seek a Second Opinion

Before seeking a second opinion, the patient should ask himself if he really needs a second opinion. It is essential to understand when not to seek a second opinion. There is a saying, "If it is not broken don't fix it." Sometimes a second opinion can lead to an avoidable tragedy. Here are a few examples to help illustrate my point.

Well-controlled epilepsy (seizure disorder) on small dosage of anti-epileptic medicine

A patient of mine with seizure disorder due to Tuberous sclerosis was well controlled on a small dose of anti-convulsant. Tuberous sclerosis (TS) is a genetic disorder, characterized by tubers (non-malignant tumours) that develop in different organs, primarily in the brain, eyes, kidney, skin and lungs. Patients frequently have hard to control seizures, developmental delay and mental retardation. On very small dose of anti-convulsant, my patient's seizures were surprisingly well controlled, allowing him to live a semi-independent life. He was able to take care of his basic needs. I had told his parents

I wonder why I slogged at medical college. Patients already know more than me from internet!

that anti-convulsant medication should continue. They sought a second opinion and a doctor told them that since their son had not suffered a seizure for a long time, anti-convulsant should be stopped. A week after stopping his anti-seizure medication, he suffered multiple seizures, one after the other (we call this status epilepticus), leading to hospitalization. He had to be intubated, put on a ventilator and medically induced into a coma to stop his seizures.

A patient on long-term steroids

Mr Smith had Addison's disease. His adrenal glands had been destroyed by tuberculosis, leading to chronic adrenal insufficiency and he was on steroid maintenance therapy for the past ten years.

Some of his relatives told him about the long term side-effects of steroids. He sought a second opinion. The second doctor, without understanding why he was on steroids, stopped the medicine. The results were disastrous. Mr Smith was rushed to the hospital in a state of shock, with no blood pressure and pulse. He almost lost his life because of the second opinion.

When you have already made up your mind on the course of action to take

Mr Jayraman is 62 years old and is my regular companion on walks. He got operated for cataract from a well known eye surgeon but felt his vision did not improve as much as he had expected. His surgeon had informed him that the operation had been performed on his lazy eye and as he had suffered solar retinitis during his childhood, his vision would not improve much, but he would perceive light better after the operation. A month later, Mr Jayraman, whose office work required the use of the computer and writing, still did not feel comfortable. He consulted the same surgeon, who informed that the cataract in his other eye was getting worse and advised surgery for it.

Mr Jayraman requested my help to get him a second opinion. I asked him two questions. First, did he feel that he needed an operation and second, did he feel comfortable with his surgeon. He answered both questions in the affirmative. I advised him if that was the case, he did not need a second opinion.

13

Second Opinion–Setting the Ball Rolling

When you plan to get a second opinion, it is a good idea to analyse your feelings and ask why you are seeking a second opinion. Are you dissatisfied with the opinion of your present doctor because:

- You think he has misdiagnosed you.
- There might be other treatment options out there.
- He did not give enough time to clear your doubts.
- He was rude, with poor bedside manners.
- He did not seem to be interested in your problem.

It is important for the patient to realize that many of these feelings may not be enough justification to seek a second opinion.

When I first joined Sir Ganga Ram Hospital, I noted that one particular specialist, Dr M, an orthopaedic surgeon, had an exceptionally big practice. His private OPD was always full of patients. One day when we were sitting together, having lunch in the hospital cafeteria, I complimented Dr M and said he must be a very gentle and affectionate doctor to attract so many patients to his practice. He looked at me for a few seconds and said,

"Why don't you come some day and see for yourself. In fact, I am rather abrupt and at times even rude with them." I did not take him up on his offer, but later came to know that this was, indeed, the case. In spite of his attitude, patients came to seek his opinion from far and near because he was a very good and competent doctor.

So a doctor who does not have the best bedside manners is not necessarily a bad doctor and reason to seek a second opinion. I know of many doctors who have poor bedside manners, but are extremely competent and are the kind of doctors I would go to if I needed a second opinion.

Patients should realize that the skill of pleasant communication is not a reflection of a doctor's competence. Few medical schools teach communication skills. However, communication skills are an important factor in medicine. Patients frequently comment, "My doctor is so gentle and compassionate that half of my disease gets cured by his words alone." Good bedside manners makes a patient comfortable in narrating his problems and even in sharing secrets about his personal life, some of which may have a bearing on the diagnosis and treatment of his ailment. If a doctor possesses both qualities, good communication skills and compassion, along with competence, he is worth his weight in gold.

14

Preparing Your Case for a Second Opinion

Having decided to seek a second opinion, a patient should prepare his or her case well before consulting the second doctor. Often, when patients come to me for a second opinion, I find them inadequately prepared. They waste time in describing trivial complaints before coming to the main problem. One patient spent 15 minutes telling me about his loss of appetite, neglecting that he had come to me regarding his gait problem which had worsened so much that he could barely walk a few yards.

I once had an opportunity to accompany a patient of mine to the United States for a second opinion. He had his case file indexed and neatly flagged. It included a concise summary of his problems, including history and investigations, from his primary physician. He had flagged the opinion of his eye specialist, endocrinologist (a specialist who deals with endocrine disorders) and urologist (a specialist who deals with problems of the urinary bladder). His investigation report was also neatly flagged. MRI and other radiological investigations were neatly arranged in separate envelopes in chronological order. The doctor consulted for the second opinion was able read the summary of the case written by his primary physician, describing his problem and the opinion from the other consultants. The American doctor was so impressed by my patient's presentation of his case that he enquired, "Are you a doctor yourself?"

So, if you plan to seek a second opinion, a good preparation is required. Time spent on the preparation of the case is worthwhile, as it helps in getting a correct answer. Take the help of your primary doctor in case preparation.

My twin is for the second opinion!

15

From Whom to Seek a Second Opinion?

After having prepared the case well, the next most important question to ask is, from whom should you seek a second opinion? Guidance of the primary physician (family doctor) is, at times, of great help as they know most specialists and can refer you to the right one. Most large hospitals have websites listing names of their doctors and their interests and expertise. In addition to a hospital website, an internet search may yield details of various specialists, along with their field of interest and competency. Many patients find out about specialists from their friends and relatives. Present and past patients of a doctor are an excellent resource and can yield useful information. Their feedback can usually be depended upon.

16
Choosing the Right Consultant

It is very important that, when you are planning to take a second opinion, you choose the right consultant. It may sound simple and obvious, but it can be a very difficult task. Let me illustrate with an example.

When my daughter, Neetika, got married, my wife, Shashi, organized a party to welcome her in-laws to our home. We did not have much help, so Shashi was running around making all the necessary arrangements. She wanted everything to be perfect. In her haste, she slipped and sprained her left knee. In spite of her injury, she continued to work to make the party a success. After the party, she suffered from regular knee pain. Pain killers helped somewhat, but the pain would come back. So followed consultations with a couple of orthopaedic surgeons, especially those with expertise in injuries of the knee.

Her MRI of the knee was interpreted as questionable medial meniscus tear. I must emphasize this was 16 years ago, when MRI technology was still nascent in India. At that time knee arthroscopy was very popular. I consulted two leading knee surgeons, both of whom I knew well. Both advised immediate knee arthroscopy and meniscus repair. Shashi, herself a doctor, was not too keen on undergoing surgery. So over next three months she was on conservative treatment, with analgesics for pain relief and physiotherapy. Her pain would settle down, only to return after some time. Ultimately, she decided to get arthroscopic knee surgery done.

As she was being wheeled into surgery, I was having second thoughts. However, the surgery went ahead as planned. Following the operation, she had postoperative pain and swelling in her left knee joint, which settled down in 2-3 weeks. Her knee, though, continued to bother her and she had great difficulty in climbing stairs. I then took her to London and consulted a leading orthopaedic surgeon at Cromwell Hospital. He opined that her pain was due to marked osteoarthritis in the knee and threw a hint that it was complicated by the arthroscopic surgery.

Back in Delhi, we kept going to the doctor who had done the arthroscopy and he kept assuring us that she needed periodic analgesics and physiotherapy only. My son, Nitin, who is a neurologist in New York, also felt reassured after hearing this. A couple of my doctor friends, though, suggested knee replacement surgery. But whenever we discussed this with our doctor, he would reassure us that there was no need for it.

Because of her knee problem, Shashi's social life was curtailed. Her cousin in Jaipur had undergone a successful knee surgery and was leading a full life. She convinced Shashi that she should get knee replacement surgery.

One day Shashi surprised me by insisting on knee replacement surgery. I took her to Sir Ganga Ram Hospital to Doctor N for consultation. After examining her, he advised knee replacement surgery. He enquired why we had waited so long. The knee problem had now affected her hip also. He also assured us that Shashi would have a good outcome.

A successful surgery was, indeed, carried out and after that Shashi became pain free and started walking better. I realized that in spite of being doctors ourselves, we had consulted the wrong consultants. Doctor B, Shashi's first knee surgeon, only specialized in arthroscopy, not knee replacement surgery. Many a times a doctor' advice is biased by his specialization. Hence, the importance of choosing the right consultant.

In *Practical Neurology* in 2010, Dr Gerald Stern wrote an excellent article titled *Finding the Right Consultant*. He described a situation in 1994, when after a tiring day at the World Congress of Neurology, he found himself in the company of two famous neurologists—Late Dr David Marsden and Dr Eldad Melamed. During the conversation, he was entrusted with the task of determining the gestational period of an elephant. In his own words, this simple task proved to be exceedingly difficult. His search for the right answer took him to consult a renowned professor of zoology, only to draw a blank. He was equally disappointed when he contacted the Director of the London Zoological Society. In the end he contacted the keeper of the zoo elephants, a Mr O'Reilly, who not only gave him the exact information, but added that it is important to distinguish between male and female calves.

So it is very important to consult the right doctor. A majority of times this is the doctor who has extensive experience with the diagnosis and treatment of the illness that plagues you.

17

Who is the Best Physician?

The Art of War is an ancient Chinese military treatise attributed to Sun Tzu, a high-ranking military general, strategist and tactician. A definitive work on military strategy and tactics of its time, it still influences Eastern and Western military thinking, business tactics, legal strategy and more. The first annotated English language translation was completed and published by Lionel Giles in 1910. Leaders as diverse as Mao Zedong and General Douglas MacArthur drew inspiration from this work. Following is an excerpt from the book, *The Art of War*, translated by Thomas Cleary:

> According to an old story, a lord in ancient China asked his physician, a member of a family of healers, which of them was the most skilled in the art. The physician, whose reputation was such that his name was synonymous with medical names in China, replied, "My eldest brother sees the spirit of sickness and removes it before it takes shape. So his name does not get out of the house. My elder brother cures sickness when it is still extremely minute and his name does not get out from the neighbourhood. As for me, I puncture veins, prescribe potions and massage skin. So from time to time my name gets out and is heard among the lords."

As in the story of the ancient healers, in Sun Tzu's philosophy, the peak efficiency of knowledge and strategy is to make conflict altogether unnecessary — to overcome the other army without fighting is the best of skills. A good physician is one who spends time to advise his patients how to keep healthy and prevent the occurrence of disease. The best physician is one who recognizes the disease in the early stages itself and acts in time to make the "combat" of the disease unnecessary.

So when my patients ask for a second opinion, I guide them not only to the right consultant, but also the best physician. Unfortunately, for a patient to determine who is the best doctor is not an easy task and they frequently get swayed by paid advertisements or impressive list of degrees behind a doctor's name. Frequently, the best physician is one who never pays to advertise and hence may not be so well known outside the confines of the hospital he practises in.

18

When to Take a Second Opinion?

Having discussed when not to seek a second opinion, it is also important to know when a second opinion should be taken. You should seek a second opinion under the following circumstances:

- Difficulty in diagnosis or if the diagnosis is uncertain or ambivalent.
- Symptoms not improving with the current treatment.
- When the diagnosis is confirmed but multiple treatment options are available. So the question is, which one to pursue?
- Unexplainable or out-of-range laboratory or imaging result.
- When an intervention or surgery is recommended.
- When an incurable disease has been diagnosed.
- Seeming to order more investigations than relevant to the problem.

I will take up each point one by one.

Difficulty in diagnosis or if the diagnosis is uncertain or ambivalent

It is a good practice to ask your doctor what is wrong with you or what the diagnosis is. Surprisingly, many patients do not ask this either out of hesitation or fear. The hesitation arises as they fear it may offend their doctor or they fear about hearing an unpleasant diagnosis.

So patients do not ask what is wrong with them and many doctors do not discuss the diagnosis with their patients and simply say, "Take these medicines and you shall become better." Trust is great, but it is always good to know what is wrong with your health. I know of friends and colleagues who are scared of undergoing routine laboratory tests in case something like diabetes is found and they may have to take medicines lifelong. They would rather not take the tests and live in denial. I also have patients who want to know their diagnosis in detail and everything else about it. On their subsequent office visit, they may want to clear additional doubts as they have read up on the subject on the internet. In the process, they get more and more confused and worried, thinking of all the possible horrible complications which could happen. Both these extreme attitudes are unhealthy.

Do not get upset or concerned if the doctor talks of a number of possible diagnoses or the diagnosis is uncertain

Sometimes, it is impossible for a doctor to give a firm diagnosis right at the onset, as the disease may still be developing and all signs and symptoms may not have manifested. So he may only give you a possible or probable diagnosis. For example, if you consult a doctor about fever accompanied by itchiness in the throat and body aches, he may say, "I think you are coming down with the flu," and ask you to take rest. You then ask him if it is swine flu since you have read in the newspapers that swine flu is prevalent. If you do not get a straight answer, there is no reason to panic and rush for a second opinion. Most diseases are brief and self-limiting. It is possible that, on your second visit, when the doctor has had a chance to review your condition and the laboratory tests, he may be in a better position to be more specific about the diagnosis.

Let me illustrate this by narrating two cases.

A patient with multiple symptoms

A 38-year-old lady, with fever for ten days, developed chills and jaundice and had to be hospitalized under the care of a gastroenterologist. She was investigated and treated for fever and jaundice, but her condition did not improve. Tests for viral markers for hepatitis were negative. She became confused and delirious. That was when the family requested a second opinion from me. The patient was febrile, looking sick and her jaundice was increasing. She was irritable and confused, but there was no neck stiffness present. Absence of neck stiffness ruled out meningitis. The blood counts were in normal range and blood cultures negative. Generally, in viral hepatitis, by the time jaundice develops, the fever starts to subside. In this case the fever was not only persisting, but was accompanied with chills and rigor. In tropical countries, malaria occurs with chills and rigor. Jaundice can occur in complicated cases of malaria when the liver is affected. Moreover, in malaria the blood counts and blood culture will be normal. Complicated malaria may affect more than one organ, as was happening in this case initially, with liver being affected, followed by the brain in the form of confusion and irritability. A close look at investigations revealed that the kidney seemed to be affected also, with rise in creatinine and blood urea nitrogen.

I discussed my diagnosis with the treating physician and her family, ordered repeated blood smears for identification of malaria parasite and started the patient on anti-malaria drug therapy. There was no time to wait for the results of investigation and the patient's condition deteriorated within two hours of starting treatment. She developed seizures and had to be shifted to the ICU and intubated. Treatment along the lines of complicated malaria continued. Mercifully, after 24 hours, one blood sample came back positive for Falciform malaria. Everyone felt reassured about my diagnosis. It was only after 48 hours that she started responding, came off the respirator and gradually recovered.

A patient with pyrexia of unknown origin

A 40-year-old man was in the hospital after being diagnosed with pyrexia (fever) of unknown origin (PUO). Four weeks had already passed and in spite of extensive investigation, no specific diagnosis was reached. I was called to render a second opinion as the patient had developed slight weakness in one leg and was retaining urine. PUO is always a clinical challenge. Examination revealed low grade fever. He was looking weak and rundown, with slight weakness in both legs. Below the nipples he felt less sensation. My detailed examination revealed that he had mild stiffness of the neck. Neck stiffness suggested meningitis, weakness in the legs, urine retention and a sensory level suggested spinal cord involvement. So he had meningo-myelitis, an inflammation of meningitis with involvement of the spinal cord. All other investigations were normal, except ESR (sedimentation rate), which was very high. A lumbar puncture (spinal tap) was done and examination of the fluid confirmed meningitis and suggested tuberculosis. Appropriate treatment with anti-tubercular drugs was immediately started.

The above are two examples where a second opinion helped to establish the correct diagnosis and initiate proper treatment.

Remember self-diagnosis may lead to grief.

I already diagnosed myself from Google and Yahoo. I am here for a second opinion!

Too often, patients do not even seek a first opinion and self-diagnosis is quite common. Recently, on a visit to the United States, I phoned my cousin to enquire about his health. He said he was doing well, but his wife had developed a "large heart" due to thyroid disease and high blood pressure. I asked him how the thyroid dysfunction and blood pressure went unnoticed so long and reached this stage. They had not seen any doctor for a health check-up for the past two years. During that period, she had put on weight and started complaining of breathlessness on exertion. Even these symptoms did not ring any alarm bells. I asked him why they had ignored this and he replied, "We thought that the breathlessness was due to overweight." I remember my cousin's wife used to be lean and thin. So I asked him, "Why did you not get her investigated for being overweight, maybe hypothyroidism would have been diagnosed at that time." He simply said, "We assumed the weight gain was post-menopausal and a result of advancing age."

This is a great example of the problem of self-diagnosis—not even consulting a primary physician till the damage is already done. The lady now had developed heart problems because she ignored her spells of breathlessness. I wish my cousin had understood the importance of routine annual medical check-ups. I wish he had paid attention when his wife was gaining weight and had consulted a doctor, instead of assuming that it was post-menopausal. I wish alarm bells had rung when she complained of her first spell of breathlessness, instead of assuming that it was due to obesity. These myths and assumptions prevail in society and self-diagnosis is a common and dangerous ailment.

When diagnosis is made but confirmation is awaited

A 22-year-old lady was referred by an eye specialist for sudden blurring of vision in her right eye. Optic neuritis (inflammation of the optic nerve) was suspected and the eye specialist advised her to seek the opinion of a neurologist. After reviewing her history in detail and examining her, I also opined that she had optic neuritis. In optic neuritis, the myelin covering of the optic nerve gets inflamed and de-myelinated, which causes blurring and loss of vision. I ordered tests, including visual evoked potential (VEP) and MRI. Both tests confirmed the diagnosis of optic neuritis. MRI showed swelling of the optic nerve behind the eye. In addition, the MRI showed two hyper-intense lesions in the right upper part of the brain. Spine MRI was normal. MRI with hyper-intense lesions raised the probability that she may develop multiple sclerosis in the future. The question was whether I should inform her about this, as it would cause her anxiety. Not informing her, on the other hand, would be professionally unethical.

I told her that she had optic neuritis which would respond very well to steroids. I delicately told her of the probability of multiple sclerosis developing in the future. She seemed to take it in her stride. But on her next visit, although her visual symptoms had improved, she appeared agitated as she had read on the internet about multiple sclerosis. She now had "cyberchondria" (escalation of concerns about common symptoms based on review of search results and literature online) and imagined that she might suffer all the severe consequences of multiple sclerosis. The fact that she was engaged to be married soon also heightened her anxiety.

Medical problems sometimes have deep social implications which are difficult to handle. The doctor has to be humane and scientifically correct at the same time. I suggested that if she wanted to seek a second opinion, she could consult one my colleagues. I gave her the names of a few good neurologists who I knew would give her sound medical advice.

An astute physician, after detailed clinical examination and relevant investigations, makes a presumptive clinical diagnosis and starts treating the patient. If he did not do so, 80 per cent of the cases would not be treated or the symptoms would become more severe. For an exact diagnosis, the doctor requires histopathological or bacteriological confirmation, which may not be possible or feasible in every case. Let me give another example.

Another patient with fever

A 30-year-old man was having low-grade fever, mostly in the evenings, for the past six weeks, with no chills or rigors. Initially, for the first two weeks, he was not bothered about it. But as the fever persisted, he consulted his physician who gave him a check-up, but did not find anything abnormal. The physician ordered blood tests and advised him to take Crocin 500 mg (Tylenol) as and when required. The test reports showed the patient's blood counts as normal, ESR and sedimentation rate was high at 40, while the blood and urine cultures were reported normal. After a week or so, on his next visit, the patient, on being questioned by the physician, admitted having a cough, but no phlegm or expectoration. He also complained of feeling weak. A detailed physical examination again did not reveal any abnormality. A chest X-ray revealed slight haziness or infiltration in the right upper zone of the chest, indicative of pulmonary tuberculosis.

In India, low-grade fever with evening rise of temperature for over four weeks, high ESR with right upper-zone infiltration in the chest X-ray, certainly raises concern for pulmonary tuberculosis. For many physicians, this may be enough to start the patient on anti-tuberculosis treatment. A bacteriological confirmation of acid fast bacilli (AFB) in the sputum would confirm the diagnosis of tuberculosis.

The patient was having a mild cough, but was not bringing out any sputum. The patient was asked to cough deeply and his sputum was collected for three days for AFB testing. If the sample was found positive for AFB, the diagnosis would be confirmed. As these tests were inconclusive, the patient was advised to undergo bronchoscopy, where a small tube is inserted in the bronchus under local anaesthesia and bronchoscopy lavage is done. If AFB is seen in the lavage, it confirms the diagnosis. If the results are still negative, the diagnosis remains clinical and the doctor may treat the patient with anti-tubercular therapy empirically. In some patients a chest CT scan may show hilar lymphadenopathy and it may be possible to get a CT-guided biopsy from a hilar lymph node. The biopsy may confirm the diagnosis of tuberculosis.

The above case highlights that sometimes it is not possible to make a definite diagnosis without confirmation with either bacteriological or histopathological data. The patient should be aware of these limitations before seeking a second opinion.

What does a patient do in such situation?

It is always advisable to ask your doctor, "What is wrong with me, doctor. What is the diagnosis?" Depending on the answer your doctor gives, you will know how sure the doctor is of the diagnosis.

These questions may upset some doctors. So it may be better to frame your question as, "Is my diagnosis confirmed?" Don't hesitate to ask pointed questions regarding your disease, including whether the diagnosis is a probability or a certainty. It is always better to be aware of your diagnosis than to remain in the dark. Ask more questions, politely, if you are not satisfied. The additional information may help you in looking after your health better.

If you still feel unsatisfied or feel that the diagnosis is doubtful, it is time to seek a second opinion. It is always a good idea to ask your doctor if he feels you should have a second opinion and if so, who he would suggest. Or you can go back to your primary physician and discuss your misgivings with him. He may be in a position to explain things more satisfactorily. He may also talk to the specialists and then clear your doubts or he may refer you to another specialist.

Symptoms not improving with the current treatment

If you are not improving with the medications prescribed, it becomes a matter of concern. The first question that you should ask is whether the diagnosis is correct. Before asking that question, there are few other possibilities one should know.

Mismatch of expectations and natural course of disease

A 55-year-old man came to me seeking a second opinion. He had suffered an ischemic stroke, leading to weakness of the left side of his body due to blockage of the right middle cerebral artery. He was upset that even after one week of treatment his weakness had not improved. I knew this was a case of a mismatch between the patient's expectations and the expected course of the disease after a stroke. The neurologist had not explained to him that recovery would take time, maybe several months or even a year. I informed him that had he come within the "therapeutic window," that is, within three hours of the onset of the stroke, he would have been a candidate for administration of tPA, a clot buster drug that may lead to rapid recovery from an ischemic stroke. But as he had arrived late, he was not given tPA and was rightly administered medicine to control his blood pressure, diabetes and high cholesterol. He would need good physiotherapy and recovery would be gradual and at times incomplete. It is better for a patient to ask his doctor why he is not improving, before seeking a second opinion.

Mismatch between a doctor's statement and the patient's understanding — Cure vs Control

A 14-year-old Sikh boy came to me for a second opinion for refractory epilepsy (seizures not controlled with medications). He had tried several anti-seizure medicines, but his seizures continued. He had undergone numerous EEGs and MRI scans. As I went through his medical records, one thing struck me. During the initial two-and-a-half-years, his seizures were well controlled with carbamazepine (a seizure medication). After that he was put on several anti-seizure medicines, but none controlled his seizures. I asked his mother the reason for stopping carbamazepine when it was clearly working for him. She said a doctor told the family about new anti-seizure medicines which were better than the old ones and switched him over to a new medicine.

After that, at regular intervals, new anti-seizure medicines were introduced by the doctor. I asked the mother why she allowed that to happen and she said she was hoping that the new anti-seizure medicine would cure her son of epilepsy. I was dumbfounded. I was upset with the treating doctor as I feel he gave the family false hope. There was also clearly a disconnect between the doctor's statement and the mother's understanding. He, most likely, was talking about controlling the seizures, while she was seeking a permanent cure for her son's disorder.

A new medicine may not necessarily be the best medicine.

Therapy may take time to act

I described earlier a patient who had low-grade fever recurring every evening, with high ESR and upper zone lung infiltration. When the doctor starts a patient on anti-tubercular therapy, the fever may persist although the patient starts feeling better. This, generally, occurs in patients with tuberculous lymph node enlargement, which can take considerable time to subside. So if therapy is not working as expected, first ask your doctor the reason. The doctor may be able to explain when the disease will respond to the treatment.

There could be no response to the therapy in spite of the right diagnosis due to drug resistance. This usually occurs in bacterial infections if the bacteria are resistant to the antibiotic. A change of therapy is then needed. So ask your doctor about this before rushing to seek a second opinion.

When the diagnosis is confirmed but multiple treatment options are available

In clinical practice, situations arise where the diagnosis is confirmed but there are multiple treatment options available. How to choose which one is the best?

Often, a patient may want a second opinion before making the choice. My brother experienced pain in the chest, discomfort, restlessness, breathlessness and sweating, one night. His wife rushed him to a nearby nursing home, where he was diagnosed to have suffered a heart attack. He recovered and was discharged and advised to get angiography done at a bigger hospital.

My brother and his wife are both doctors. My brother was completely shaken by the heart attack. But as the days passed, he regained confidence and started taking care of his health, with medication, change of lifestyle, going for walks and dietary modification. He was not willing to go for angiography and was scared as he felt it would be followed by an angioplasty or bypass. Two invasive cardiologists suggested immediate cardiac angiography. A third senior non-invasive cardiologist was not very enthusiastic about angiography.

Heads it is surgery, tails it is a placebo!

Ultimately, he underwent a radionuclide angiography (MUGA Scan) test which suggested that he had suffered a mild heart attack and that there was no reversible cardiac ischemia. Luckily, at that time a study appeared in the New England Journal of Medicine, studying a large number of such cases. In UK, most of the cardiologists favoured a less aggressive approach, while in USA most centres were pursuing an aggressive approach. Results were equally good with the aggressive, as also the conservative approach. When I showed this article to them, the differences of opinion between husband and wife abated. My brother, a general physician, was scared of angiography. His wife, also a doctor, was insisting on angiography as she worried about her husband's health. Both were right in their own way.

> *Medicine is not a perfect science, there are areas of probabilities, not always certainty.*
>
> *As medicine is not perfect science, don't expect your doctor to be God; he may help you to make a choice, but he cannot predict the future.*

Unexplainable or out-of-range laboratory or imaging results

My brother, who lives in the United States, during his annual medical check-up found that his Prostate Specific Antigen (PSA) was high. It had gone from 2 to 3.4 and now was 5.6. He was concerned when it rose to 5.6 as the normal upper limit is 4. He discussed this abnormal result with his primary care physician who advised him to repeat his PSAs after two or three months. My brother, dissatisfied with that answer, consulted a urologist. Though per rectum examination was normal, the urologist advised him to get a prostate biopsy. This upset my brother, as he was seeking reassurance from the urologist. He rang up my nephew, who is practicing as an internist in Chicago. My nephew advised him against surgical intervention, saying urologists are fond of advising interventional procedure. Now my brother felt reassured.

At that time I visited USA and my brother, accompanied by his two sons, came to meet me in New York. My son, who is a neurologist in New York, was present and convinced my brother that since he was only 55 years of age and the PSA was trending up, he needed to go for a biopsy immediately. He explained to him that if he was older (70 and above), he would have advised against the procedure. My brother went back to his urologist and underwent biopsy of the prostate. In the biopsy report, 3 specimens out of 12 showed cancer and he was advised surgical removal of the prostate. My brother took a second opinion from another urologist in Pennsylvania, who also recommended surgery. He told my brother that after the operation he may experience temporarily incontinence and impotency. Robotic surgery was less invasive than open surgery, with less risk of impotency.

My brother decided to take the opinion of two more urologists in New York, Dr T who specialized in robotic surgery and Dr H who did both open and robotic surgery. Dr H told him that in case robotic surgery was unsuccessful, he would switch to open surgery. Dr T, who did four robotic operations per day and had a lot of experience, advised my brother to have an endorectal ultrasound, the results of which were negative for prostate cancer. My brother was now confused. Scared of an operation, he even considered repeating the biopsy. Finally, he underwent robotic surgery successfully.

Everyone panics when an unexplained and abnormal (out of range) laboratory or imaging test is detected and concern for a serious medical problem like cancer is raised. Getting a second opinion at this juncture is justified, especially if your physician cannot explain the abnormal test result to your satisfaction. But be diplomatic. Do not upset your physician or surgeon as you seek a second or third opinion, since at some stage you may need their services.

A lab result needs to be correlated with clinical history.

Histopathology tissue and slides, and second opinion

Arthur Hailey wrote a book, *The Final Diagnosis*, which outlines the role of a pathologist in making the final diagnosis. A correct pathological report is vital to determine treatment options. Conversely, an incorrect report can have disastrous consequences. So many patients, who are diagnosed with cancer, seek a second opinion on their pathology specimen. This helps to confirm the diagnosis and guide treatment forward. I recommend in these cases that patients or their family members seek a second opinion from a reputed pathologist. Pathologists in renowned cancer centres (both in Indian and abroad such as Memorial Sloan Kettering Cancer Center in New York) are available to consult in difficult cases.

When an intervention or surgery is recommended

A patient may want to have a second opinion when an intervention or surgery is suggested. One of my friends in New York, Dr Josh Torgovnick, tells his patients, "You can always operate, but you can never un-operate." So if surgery is suggested and there is time (meaning, it is not an emergency surgery), seek a second opinion.

When an incurable disease has been diagnosed

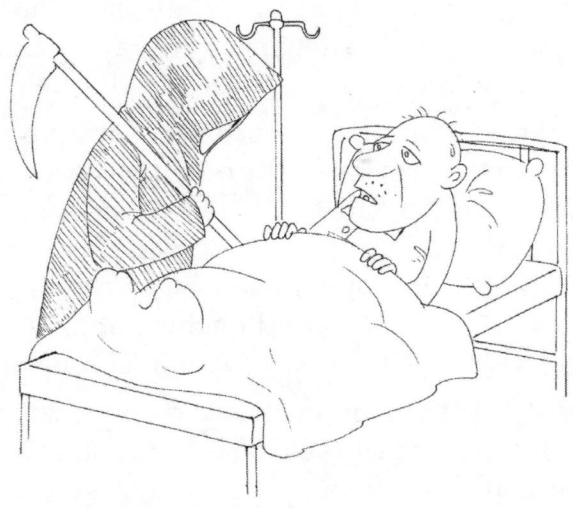

How much for a second opinion?

A second opinion is a must if a person is diagnosed with an incurable disease. There are always doubts whether the diagnosis is correct. Is the evidence for the incurable disease strong and irrefutable? Is something missing? Even if diagnosis is correct, is it true that there is no treatment available? All these questions come to the mind of the patient.

As I have stated earlier, medicine is not a perfect science. There are diseases which mimic each other in their clinical presentation. Diagnostic errors can, and do, occur. As a neurologist, I double-check the clinical history, examination and relevant investigations before diagnosing my patient with amytrophic lateral sclerosis (ALS), also called motor neuron disease (MND), a disease with no cure. I do not hesitate to advise the patient to seek another opinion. I observe the patient carefully for progression of the disease and repeat investigations such as electromyography (EMG) to confirm the diagnosis.

Dementia is another neurodegenerative disease which has no cure. But all dementia cases are not Alzheimer disease and some dementias are curable. So thorough investigations are needed so as not to miss a curable cause of dementia, such as vitamin B12 deficiency. Therefore, second or third opinions are all justifiable when confronted with an incurable disease.

Having identified an incurable disease, you should understand that an incurable disease can still be treated. The treatment helps to make the patient's life pain-free and as comfortable as possible. A lot of research is ongoing and diseases which are incurable today may be curable in the future. So the patient should not lose hope. Many cancers which, till recently, had a very poor prognosis can now be treated and the patient's life extended.

Some patients with incurable diseases seek relief and possibly cure through alternate medicine. A large number of such patients, even from advanced western countries, go to China for stem cell therapy and other alternate therapies, many of which do not meet FDA recommendations. In a majority of cases, the patient loses his money and remains without a cure. A second opinion may help such patients and help to put things in a proper perspective. False hope is not good and the second opinion may prevent the patient from getting cheated. He can face reality in a peaceful manner by putting his finances and property in order and spend the remainder of his life doing things he always wanted to do. He can also plan for end of life issues and write a living will.

Seeming to order more investigations than relevant to the problem

If you feel this, you may ask the doctor politely how these investigations will help your primary problem. He will explain to you why these investigations are being asked for. If still in doubt, you have a second opinion regarding this.

When too many heart investigations were being ordered, a lady, in a humorous way, quipped, "Doctor, doctor, I have a headache, not a heartache!"

19

Second Opinion in Surgery or Intervention

You may take an opinion from another surgeon or interventionist in that field. This may help you make up your mind, but it would be still better to take a second opinion from a physician specializing in the same field. For example, if the opinion of a cardiac surgeon is to go for a bypass, you should get the opinion of a good non-invasive cardiologist whether he, too, recommends surgery. Surgeons, as we say in medicine, love to operate! So if a neurosurgeon tells you that you need surgery, sometimes the opinion of a neurologist is helpful in reassuring you that you are on the right path.

A speciality where there are only surgeons but no corresponding physicians

My CA (charted accountant), Mr RP, asked me to see his cousin's mother who had recently suffered a stroke, resulting in paralysis of her left side, following surgery for fracture of her femur. This 78-year-old lady, with hypertension and diabetes, had been operated upon four years earlier, successfully, for a fracture of the neck of the right femur. After the operation, she was active and mobile. About a year earlier, she slipped and fell again and suffered a fracture, this time of the neck of her left femur. This time she opted not to get operated. She gradually recovered and started walking, but with a limp. She was in USA, living with her elder son and moved to Delhi to live with her younger son.

Seeing her limping and hobbling, her younger son sought the help of an orthopaedic surgeon who, after getting an X-ray, told him that the neck of the femur was united, but with an angulation. He suggested surgery to straighten the angulation so that she could walk properly.

Immediately after the operation, she suffered a stroke on same side as the operation, as a result of which she was not able to walk at all. Earlier, she was walking and doing her daily chores. Now she was totally paralysed.

I was upset and asked my CA why his cousin had not taken another opinion. His answer surprised me. He had taken an opinion from another orthopaedic surgeon, who had also recommended surgery. This was the first time I became aware that orthopaedic surgeons did not have any counterpart orthopaedic physicians, someone who could give an unbiased opinion about the need for surgery.

Rupture rotator cuff of shoulder

Dr AC, my cardiologist colleague in the hospital, fell while dancing and tore his right rotator cuff. He was in severe pain and unable to lift his arm above the shoulder. He consulted his colleagues and decided to undergo surgery by a reputed surgeon in Mumbai. After the operation, his shoulder was strapped to his waist and he underwent intensive physiotherapy for eight weeks. Even after 12 weeks of physiotherapy, he had shoulder pain and was unable to lift his arm completely up to the shoulder. A year later he fell again, rupturing his left rotator cuff. He again went through surgery, again with the same post-operative results. At the same time, another doctor-colleague in the same hospital, an eye surgeon, Dr R, had a rupture of the right rotator cuff. He also went to Mumbai to consult the same surgeon, but chose medical therapy with analgesics and intensive physiotherapy. I had discouraged him from undergoing surgery. He gradually improved and after six months had full movements of his shoulder. Every time I met him, he would enthusiastically raise his arm above his shoulder, showing that he had fully recovered without surgery.

The moral of story is that nature has given our body immense power for recovery, provided we remain patient and do appropriate physiotherapy and exercises. Surgery is not always the right action.

When the luxury of a relaxed, well-planned second opinion does not exist

With the advances in cardiology, the approach to treatment in cases of cardiac emergencies has changed. As soon as you have symptoms of a heart attack, such as discomfort in the chest or sweating, you are rushed off to hospital in an ambulance. In the hospital you will be immediately attended to by doctors and undergo ECG and blood tests. If need be, you are rushed to the cardiac laboratory for a cardiac angiography. In case of a major coronary artery block or triple-vessel block, you have to decide whether you want to opt for cardiac stent or coronary bypass. This is while you are still in the cardiac lab with a catheter in your heart. Taking a decision at that time is not easy, in spite of the explanation given by the attending cardiologist. There is no time to waste, the decision has to be quick and there is no time for a second opinion.

A timely angioplasty may save your heart from a major heart attack. Either you accept whatever your attending cardiologist advises or you make your own decision if you have knowledge of such things. Some knowledge is acquired from friends who have faced this problem, provided you paid attention when they described their situation. So you learn from the experiences of others or acquire knowledge by reading on this subject.

Most of us are not curious enough to learn from the experiences of others or feel that it was their "misfortune" as they were not "looking after" their health". On other hand, you feel that your "karma" is good, so "nothing bad" will happen to you.

In certain conditions, surgery is a must as it makes a difference between life and death

A large subdural hematoma (collection of blood outside the brain, but inside the skull) of the brain, if not operated upon in time, can compress the brain stem irreversibly, leading to brain death. Subarachnoid haemorrhage (bleeding from a ruptured aneurysm) can be fatal if not surgically attended to in time. A ruptured peptic ulcer needs urgent intervention. A ruptured intestine or appendix, similarly calls for immediate intervention.

Intervention or no intervention, surgery or no surgery, timely decisions have to be made. There are no dictums. One thing is sure, a good opinion may help to guide you through crisis.

20

Multiple Second Opinions and Medical Shopping

I never do anything without a third opinion!

Some patients seek multiple opinions about their medical problems as if they are on a shopping spree. Why do they do that? Maybe they are looking for some doctor who may endorse their beliefs or want to avoid an operation or intervention or remain unconvinced about the right treatment option. Where does this stop?

This is sometimes referred to as doctor shopping.

However, there are times when doctor shopping may actually help. Some years ago, I was consulted by a leading industrialist. Mr S was experiencing difficulty in walking. He did not feel as steady as he did earlier. He had a history of mild hypertension, which was well controlled with anti-hypertensive medicine. His blood sugar was borderline high and controlled with exercise and dietary modification. He had mild hyperlipidemia (high cholesterol), for which he was on medicine. He had a history of heart disease and was on anti-platelet medication. Examination revealed that he was experiencing difficulty walking in a straight line, heel to toe. He could stand on either leg, but was unable to hop on one leg. Ankle jerks could not be obtained. Examination suggested mild peripheral neuropathy as the cause of his walking problem.

Diabetes was thought to be responsible for his peripheral neuropathy. But there was a surprise waiting for me. He had already had a MRI brain scan, which showed a large meningioma, a benign brain tumour extending from the base of his brain, wrapping around the optic nerve and chiasma and extending down the brain stem with mildly dilated ventricles, with mild cortical atrophy. Now the question was, what part was this playing in his walking difficulty and what to do about it.

My impression was that the meningioma was not the cause of his walking difficulty. I was unsure how to treat his large tumour. Operating such a large meningioma in a man of his age was not without risk. On the other hand, as the meningioma was wrapped around the optic chaisma and nerve and if not operated, he risked loss of vision.

Then started a series of second opinions. The first was given by a neurosurgeon, Dr K, from New York, who was visiting India. Dr K was a renowned professor of neurosurgery at New York University (NYU), specializing in base-of-the-skull surgery. After examining all the data, he opined that such extension surgery was not without risk and it was not worth undertaking. Meningiomas grow very slowly and it might be years before it grew further. I was relieved to hear that a renowned neurosurgeon, specializing in this surgery, had turned down the surgery. But I also knew that Mr S was disappointed, as he was looking for someone who would operate on him and solve his problem.

After 15 days I received a call from Mr S. He planned to seek several consultations in London and the USA and invited me to accompany him as his neurologist. I gladly accepted his offer.

Our first consultation was in London's Cromwell hospital, with a radio-therapist. That was when I realized how extensively Mr S had prepared himself for theses consultations. He had planned in advance which specialist he wanted to consult and through his network of friends had appointments scheduled with leading specialists. He had one file containing a detailed medical report from his primary physician, neatly typed and indexed. He also had the medical reports and opinions of all the specialists he had consulted so far. He had also carried his latest blood reports, MRI of the brain and spine and nerve conduction studies. Mr

S's younger brother accompanied us and took detailed notes of each consultation.

In Cromwell hospital, he presented all the data to his radio-therapist, narrated his present problems, answered all the questions of the doctor and showed him the latest laboratory report and MRI of the brain. The radio-therapist suggested fractionated radiotherapy, as he believed that, if well directed, it may stop the growth of the meningioma and even shrink it.

The next consultation was with a professor of neurosurgery at Queen Square. After a careful review of the history, physical examination and investigations, the professor's answer was straightforward, that he would not recommend surgery.

Then we flew to New York and the first consultation was at New York University Hospital with Dr K again. He had also arranged consultations with another neurosurgeon and the head of radiotherapy.

The other neurosurgeon was also not keen about surgery, while the radiotherapy consultant spoke about the possibility of fractionated radiotherapy as a treatment option. Our next meeting was with an Indian born neurosurgeon, now settled in United States. He had earned a name for base-of-the-skull neurosurgery and was working in a leading hospital on Long Island, New York. He spent a lot of time analysing the data and examining the patient and suggested a limited surgery of meningioma around the optic nerve.

Next, we flew to Johns Hopkins hospital to consult the head of neurosurgery and neuro-ophthalmology. The neurosurgeon offered to operate the meningioma, after explaining the risks involved. The opinion of the neuro-ophthalmologist was extremely helpful. He studied my patient's field charting of vision which had been done in India and agreed that the field restriction present may be due to glaucoma, but made an important observation. As my patient had loss of colour sense, this meant that the optic nerve was getting involved. He felt that radiation near the optic chiasma or optic nerve was safe.

After we came back to India, Mr S requested me to write a detailed summary of all the consultations. My recommendations were as follows:

1. There was no medical therapy for the meningioma.
2. Any further wait-and-watch policy would not be right as the optic nerve was getting involved and vision was deteriorating.
3. Surgery was not a good option and three out of four surgeons were against it.
4. Even a limited surgery around the optic chiasma or nerve had risks.
5. Proactive fractionated radiotherapy (IMRT) was the best option to stop the meningioma from growing further and possibly even to shrink it.

Radiotherapy was started and Mr S underwent regular follow-up MRI brain scans every six months for the next eight years. The meningioma did not grow any further, in fact it shrunk slightly. He did not have any deterioration of vision.

The above is an example where multiple opinions, methodically and intelligently obtained, resulted in effective handling of a complex medical problem. On the other hand, doctor shopping which is seeking medical opinions from multiple physicians in a haphazard manner, without making efforts to coordinate carefully, should be avoided since it leads to confusion about the diagnosis and management. "Too many cooks spoil the broth" is an idiom that fits well here.

21

Second Opinion–Faith and Closure

Having taken premature retirement from the Indian army, I was ready to settle down in private practice in civilian life. I accepted an offer to be a visiting physician in an Ayurveda hospital in NOIDA, near Delhi. This Ayurveda hospital, established by the world-famous Maharishi Mahesh Yogi, was a 600-bed sprawling complex. From outside, the patient rooms resembled small huts, but they were very comfortable inside. The Maharishi had recruited Ayurveda doctors, called Vaidyas, to treat the patients under the Ayurveda system of medicine.

Most of the patients were from Western countries. They either had terminal diseases or had refused allopathic treatment offered in the hospitals in the Western world. They were there to be treated under the Ayurveda system, involving a balanced diet, relaxed lifestyle, soothing chants and Ayurveda medicines administered by the Vaidyas. The patients, on arrival, would receive a special mantra individually, from either the Maharishi or one of his disciples.

I, along with another surgeon, visited the hospital twice a week. We were not expected to treat anyone, but rather to supervise the treatment being administered by the Vaidyas. My role was to periodically investigate the patients with blood tests, X-rays and CT scans in order to evaluate if their disease was responding to the Ayurveda medicines.

.On one of my visits, I met a professor of mathematics from Oxford University. He was suffering from dystonia and had been earlier treated in Queen Square by a well known specialist in movement disorder. As he did not experience relief, he came all the way from Britain to India for treatment. He told me that the sight of the earthen pots containing warm oil hanging from the ceiling and the sensation of oil dripping on his forehead gave him intense relief and satisfaction. He was happy and felt comfortable, although the treatment did not cure him of his dystonia.

There was a rich, old lady from Africa, with brain tumour, who was advised an operation in London. She flew to the USA where again she was also advised to undergo surgery. She refused and opted to be treated in India. She was scared of operations. The MRI scan revealed that her brain tumour was increasing in size, in spite of the Ayurveda medicine.

Whenever any of these patients became seriously ill and went into shock, with a drop in blood pressure or worsening clinical condition, we would rush them to the nearby modern hospital to be administered intravenous fluids, antibiotics or other supportive treatment.

One thing struck me about these terminally ill patients. They were at peace with themselves. They had colossal faith and a great sense of acceptance, even though they were away from their homes and loved ones.

When a person is terminally ill, faith is a great healer and a calming factor. This faith and acceptance may be provided by your doctor, a religious guru, a friend, a parent or a relative. Faith and acceptance are the important qualities a doctor must possess — also the humility to accept the outcome. A doctor must believe firmly that "I prescribe He (God) cures." This enduring faith can be provided by any system of medicine, doctor, religion or guru.